T0380990

To order additional copies of this book, contact:
Xlibris
1-888-795-4274
www.Xlibris.com
Orders@Xlibris.com

To:

From:

Message:

Given this date:

To share with family for love and memories and laughter that we all share in families together enjoy!

This is me and my Baby D.

Dedication

This is dedicated to my loving wife, Shaaron C. Jackson, as she put me on my road to success to share and bring forth our true life experience with our family dog.

Also to my aunt, Wilamina Richard, thank you for your thoughts in the past that I should one day put my drawing out to the world. Who would have thought that it would take a dog to make me put something out about life and a dog could save my life and my wife. We never know what tomorrow will bring into our life.

To our daughter, Shari Lewis, we dedicate this book to you because without your wanting a pet and then earning the funds from the Chris Rock Show to get him, this book would not have been thought of! But there is a saying that God is always preparing and getting people ready in the right places that you don't even know and you will meet them along the way!

We would also like to thank our family and friends who love Baby D well. He is back alive now at Babydalive.com@gmail.com, online bookstores, and your local bookstores too!

Ok, you don't know me but let's become friends today.

I have an interesting story and I'm going to share it with you.

Long ago, my family had a dog named Dollars. He was a Bichon. After his passing, they immediately went looking for another pet. While they were searching for a new dog in stores, guess what! They saw me in the cage playing with a red leather ball!

That was a special day for me. I got excited as they sign the paperwork to take me home as their new family pet member. That day in our own private limousine, they were thinking of a name for me when the youngest daughter Shari said, "Let's name him, Baby D!" I was a puppy and their previous dog's name started with D. When you put it together, you get 'Baby D'.

Next up, I will show you some scenes from the house and some things I love doing as a dog. I consider myself human just like my owner but in another form. I may not have always been understood but I have proven my worth by saving lives as I did. So, my big reward is to introduce myself to the world. We never called the media since we had no proof of the fire in our basement as dad was able to put the fire out.

So here I am ready to take over the world! Living large!

Sometimes, I like to go for walks on my own but the neighbors find me and they bring me back home.

One time, I came out of the yard and went for a walk. Then, a man grabbed me and put me in his car. My mom came down the street waving a flag and calling out my name, "Baby D!" Inside the car, I stood up and she saw me. She was able to get me back and we went home. I realized what I did was wrong. Strangers can be dangerous. You should never walk out on your own; this could upset the whole family.

My family left and went out to eat one night. I could smell the leather in her shoe closet so I went looking through her shoes. I found a red pair similar to the ball I used to play within the cage so I played with them and tore them into pieces. That was a big no-no! Why did I do that? When mom came home and walked into her bedroom, she didn't know if someone had robbed her or someone was just throwing stuff out of her closet. Then she noticed that pieces of her shoes were torn up and some explanation had to be done or else she was ready to get rid of me, Baby D.

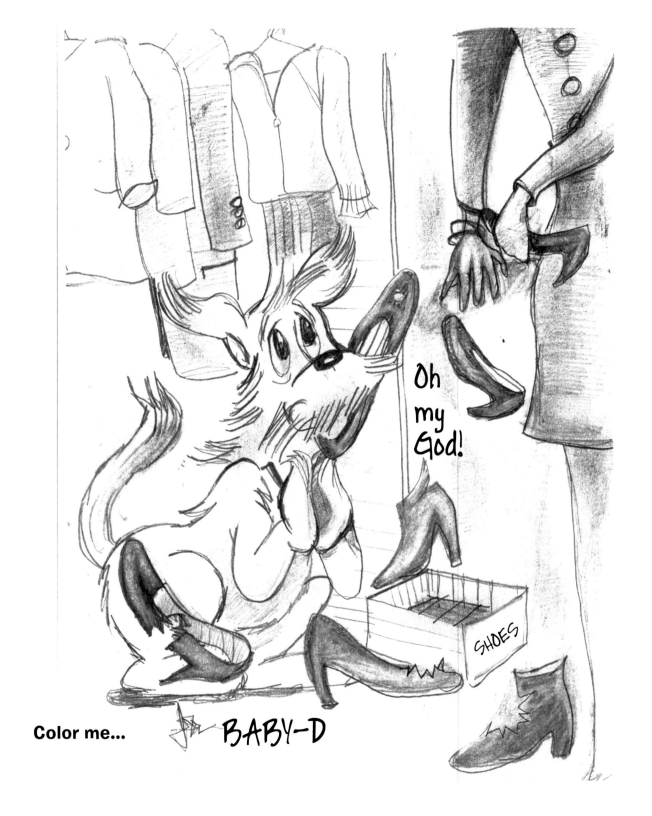

Color me...

Printed in the United States
By Bookmasters